Dinosaurs Divorce

A Guide for Changing Families

Laurie Krasny Brown and Marc Brown

LB

LITTLE, BROWN AND COMPANY

New York Boston

◈ Contents ◈

Little, Brown and Company

Hachette Book Group
237 Park Avenue, New York, NY 10017
Visit our website at www.lb-kids.com

Little, Brown and Company is a division of Hachette Book Group, Inc.
The Little, Brown name and logo are trademarks of Hachette Book Group, Inc.

First Paperback Edition: September 1988
Originally published in hardcover in October 1986 by Little, Brown and Company

Loc No. 86-1079
ISBN 978-0-316-11248-2 (hc)
ISBN 978-0-316-10996-3 (pb)

HC: 30 29 28 27 26 25 24 23 22 21
PB: 30 29 28 27 26 25
SC
Manufactured in China

TO TOLON AND TUCKER FOR SHOWING US A CHILD'S POINT OF VIEW · WITH LOVE AND THANKS FROM DAD AND LAURIE

Divorce Words and What They Mean

The starred (*) words are in the book. See if you can find them.

*divorce: A legal judgment ending a marriage. After a husband and wife get a divorce, they are both free to marry again.

*family counselor: An adult specially trained to help families solve their personal problems.

*half brother or half sister: A boy or girl born to your parent and your stepparent.

*judge: An adult with the power to hear disputes in a court of justice and to decide how they should be resolved.

*lawyer: An adult trained to help parents proceed with getting a divorce.

separation agreement: A written agreement between both parents that describes the terms by which they agree to end their marriage and the rules they will observe after their divorce. It includes rules for the following:

child custody: Describes who you will live with and who will take care of you. Custody may be granted to one parent or be shared by both parents. Occasionally, it is given to a relative or foster parent.

child support: How much money each parent will pay to help take care of you.

visiting rights: Certain times set aside for you and the parent you don't live with to be together.

alimony: Money one parent pays to the other to provide support after the divorce; usually the father pays the mother.

*stepparent: Someone who marries your mother or father after they have been divorced or one of them has died.

*stepsister or stepbrother: A girl or boy born to your stepparent and the partner your stepparent once was married to.

Why Parents Divorce

Divorce takes place between mothers and fathers. You are not to blame if your parents get divorced.

Parents divorce when they don't love each other or can't get along together anymore, no matter how hard they try.

Some parents have violent, noisy battles.

Other parents fight silently by not talking to each other.

Parents sometimes fight with you when really they are angry with each other.

Sometimes parents who are upset with each other behave in ways that hurt themselves and the rest of the family.

For these parents, it's better not to live together or be married anymore.

What About You?

When your parents divorce, it's natural to feel

sad

angry

afraid

confused

ashamed

guilty

relieved

worried about who will take care of you.

The bad feelings won't last forever, and there is plenty you can do to help yourself feel better.

It helps to talk about these feelings and to let them show.

It's okay to cry. In fact, crying can help you feel better.

If you feel angry, tell your parents why, and look for ways to show anger that don't hurt others or yourself.

If you are afraid or confused about what's happening in your family, tell your parents how you feel and ask questions.

Imagine what would happen if you kept all these feelings to yourself!

It sometimes helps to visit a family counselor who will make sure everyone gets a chance to talk and listen to each other.

Some parents can agree between themselves about who you will live with after the divorce and how often you will see each of them.

When parents can't agree, lawyers and judges decide. Try to be honest if they ask you questions; it will help them make better decisions.

After the Divorce

Divorce can bring some good changes. Your parents may feel calmer and be nicer to spend time with.

You may get to know each of them better.

You don't have to listen when parents say bad things about each other. Say you love them both and hearing this upsets you.

You may have to tell them more than once.

If parents want you to carry messages back and forth, ask them to do it themselves.

Remember divorce is new for your parents too, and they may make some mistakes.

If you move, you may have to say good-bye to friends and familiar places. But soon your new home will feel like the place you really belong.

TYRANNOSAURUS TRUCKERS
SINCE THE JURASSIC PERIOD

TOYS

Living with One Parent

Parents may need you to take care of yourself more.

You can make things easier for your parent—and yourself—if you offer to pitch in and help.

You may wish you could turn into a grown-up overnight.

But doing that isn't your job.

There may be other times when you feel like acting babyish to get attention.

Try instead to ask for some love and affection.

14

Other changes from divorce may be harder to get used to.

Living with one parent almost always means there will be less money. Be prepared to give up some things.

There will be times when you miss your other parent.

Visiting Your Parent

Visiting someone you used to live with can feel uncomfortable at first. But after a while you'll get used to it.

Your parents will want to know what you are doing in school and with your friends, about things you need help with and things that you want to do with them. Don't be shy about sharing in this way.

Some parents act like Santa Claus, always suggesting fancy or expensive things to do.

You don't have to spend lots of money to love each other and have fun together.

Some parents feel too guilty or unhappy to visit you. Sometimes you can keep in touch by calling or writing.

If not, try to spend time with other grown-ups you like and trust.

It may feel strange at first to show your love for one parent in front of the other. Try to remember it's okay to love both and to show that you do.

Having Two Homes

Spending time in two different homes can be confusing. You may feel lost or out of place. Try to find favorite things you can do with each parent.

Make a schedule to remember when you will stay at each parent's house, and keep special things in each home.

Telling one parent you have permission from the other to do something—when you don't—isn't fair to anyone. It will only get you into trouble!

The rules in each house may be different. Try to respect them in both.

Celebrating Holidays and Special Occasions

Divorce may mean twice as much celebrating at holiday times, but you may feel pulled apart.

Holidays and special occasions may not be the same. In fact, you may celebrate them in very different ways. Try to be open to these changes.

It's important to remember both your parents on holidays.

Telling Your Friends

Divorce may make you feel different from your friends.

But you're still you, no matter how many parents you live with!

CLASS, HOW MANY OF YOUR PARENTS ARE DIVORCED?

It helps to remember that you are not the only one whose parents are divorced.

It may be easier to tell your friends one at a time.

Good friends will be glad you could be honest with them.

Spending time with friends can help you feel less lonely.

Meeting Parents' New Friends

Your mother or father may go out on dates.

Staying with a baby-sitter may not be so bad.

You may sometimes feel jealous and want your parent to yourself.

Be polite to your parents' new friends, even if you don't like them at first.

Who knows? They may become friends of yours too.

25

Living with Stepparents

Divorced parents who find someone new they can love and live with happily may decide to marry again.

You may worry that stepparents are like characters in fairy tales.

But a stepparent is a grown-up who, just like you, loves your mother or father.

Most stepparents won't try to take your mother or father's place. They will care about you and want to see you happy.

You also may care about them.

Pick a name for your stepparent that you find easy to use and your step-parent is comfortable with.

Be patient. It may take a while to get used to each other's ways of doing things.

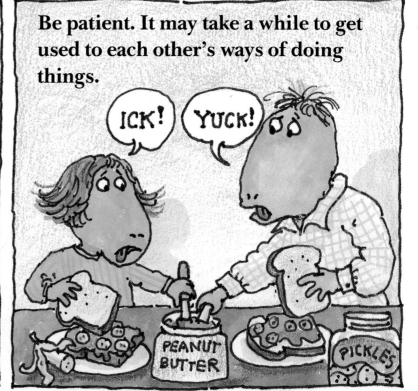

Not everyone loves his or her step-parents, but showing them respect is important.

If you do love your stepparent, be glad! It won't change the way you and your own parent feel about each other.

Having Stepsisters and Stepbrothers

Having stepparents may mean having stepbrothers and stepsisters.

You may feel invaded if you have to share a room.

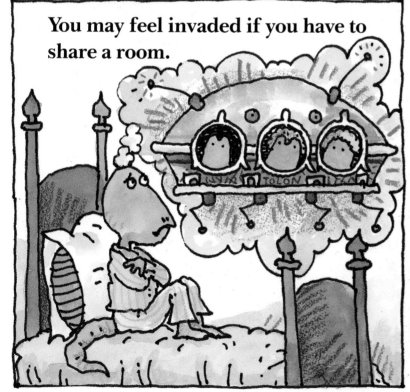

It can help to agree on spaces and things that can be private for each of you.

Learning to live with someone new takes time, so don't be surprised if there are arguments at first.

Stepbrothers and stepsisters may be good to talk to about divorce; they often have been through it too.

Finding a quiet place might take more work with a bigger family.

But, having a bigger family means there's usually someone around when you want company.

No matter how many stepsisters, stepbrothers, half sisters, or half brothers you have, your place in the family is always special.

Divorce in your family means many things will change, but one thing that never changes is your parents' love for you.